Miscarriage

Eileen McGrath, Ph.D.

RESOURCES FOR CHRISTIAN LIVING™

RESOURCES FOR FAMILIES™

Design: Karen Malzeke-McDonald

Send all inquiries to:

Resources for Families™
RCL • Resources for Christian Living™
200 East Bethany Drive
Allen, Texas 75002-3804

Toll Free   800-419-9987
Fax   800-688-8356

Printed in the United States of America

#12500   ISBN 0-7829-0752-0 Miscarriage
#12501   ISBN 0-7829-0753-9 Death of an Infant
#12502   ISBN 0-7829-0880-2 Siblings Grieve Too

2 3 4 5 6   02 01 00 99 98

ONTENTS

*I*ntroduction

During the past twenty years, I have counseled individuals who were grieving major losses in their lives. Grieving is a most distressful, painful, and an emotionally draining experience. I have learned that no one can take anyone's pain away. Empathy and support are helpful, but the person needs to feel the feelings, walk through the pain, and try to find ways to deal with the loss.

This book was written to be a companion on your journey. Your journey through grief is one of real sadness, fear, confusion, and pain. Your miscarriage is a real loss—the loss of the child growing within you, the loss of your dreams, the loss of a part of yourself—and, possibly, you feel you have lost your way. This little book is an attempt to share some insights with you. It does not presume to have all the answers to what you are experiencing, but it may offer you some direction and comfort.

I have also learned that keeping a journal, writing down your feelings, helps you to process them, feel them, and release them. Therefore, space has been provided for you to write out those feelings. There are also a few introductory open-ended sentences to start you on your way. You may not feel like writing at this time, so this space will be there if you choose to use it in the future. By keeping a journal of both good feelings and sad feelings, you are able to monitor your progress and see how you are dealing with your loss. You are also able to hope and believe that there will be good days again. Try to be gentle with yourself and know that you are not alone on your journey through grief.

Dreams

If you have been planning to have a child, the feelings of joy, wonder, and excitement engulf you when you learn you are pregnant. Sometimes feelings of fear and uncertainty can also be present. But with time you begin to dream about, imagine, and plan for this life that is growing inside of you. The bond between you and your child grows stronger every day. Your thoughts shift to the idea of being a mother. You are willing to change your lifestyle and schedule to do whatever it takes to nurture and nourish your baby. You may have waited, calculated, and planned for this precise time in your life. Your dream is unfolding.

$\mathcal{D}$reams Shattered

Mary was crying as she told me how it felt. "I had this awful feeling in the pit of my stomach. Just a little while ago, I was happy, I was pregnant, a baby was growing inside of me—my baby. Now, this terrible feeling, cramps, spotting. I knew what was happening."

The doctor confirmed Mary's suspicion: that awful feeling in the pit of her stomach was real. She had experienced a spontaneous abortion, the medical term for a miscarriage. Mary's dream was shattered. She could not believe it. She did not want to believe it. She just felt so terrible. When you experience a miscarriage, the reality begins to sink in and you realize that your dream has been destroyed. The life that was growing inside of you is ended. You may begin to feel things you have never felt before. An unbelievable sadness comes over you. You may want to scream, cry out, "Why me? Why my baby?" The tears begin to stream down your face; you feel a heaviness in your chest; you may just want to lie down and not get up. You may feel totally numb, in shock; or you may feel absolutely nothing and just find yourself staring at the wall.

Whatever the feelings that arise, just let yourself feel them. They may be like waves, washing over you at various times and with different degrees of intensity. You are grieving. Maybe you did or did not see or touch your child, and maybe you did not know if it was a boy or a girl. Nonetheless, you are sad, confused, disappointed, and you feel robbed. You did not get a chance to really know who it is you are grieving for, but you know it hurts. Your feelings are real and very normal. Others may not know how or what you are feeling. They may not understand the depth of your pain or your personal dreams and plans that you had for your child. Sometimes those closest to you really do not know what to say to comfort you. Sometimes they use clichés such as "It's okay, you can have another one," "You can get pregnant again," "It must have been God's will." Sometimes they do not want to talk about it at all, and some may be able to just listen to you. If you can, share your feelings with those you love and trust. Tell them how sad and disappointed you are and how very much it hurts.

Grief

Grieving is a process, a spiral of ups and downs. The feelings you are experiencing are all part of that process. Grief is universal, yet each of us experiences it in a unique way. You feel what you feel. Grief is about facing the pain you suffer after a loss. Grief is hard and painful and it takes time and work. There are no shortcuts and no magical ways around grief; you must walk through it.

Most of your grieving is done in private; but if you can, try to reach out to others and share what you feel. Ask for what you need and you may not experience that intense loneliness and isolation. Having a support system around you can help you feel loved and comforted. It also lets others support you when you are feeling so vulnerable.

If you are a single woman, you probably have already been through the gamut of emotions about being pregnant. This miscarriage was not a part of your plan, and it may have left you in shock and feeling very much alone. During pregnancy you were not alone; you had started to bond with your child.

Now you are alone, and it is important for you to reach out to someone with whom you can share.

Any woman, married or single, needs as much support as possible. Maybe you know someone who has had a miscarriage. If so, call and share with that person. There may be a hospital or a community-based support group for those who have experienced a fetal death. Try to connect with others, because building a wall around yourself does not isolate you from the pain but cements it inside of you.

As you continue to read this book, you will find journal space for your personal reflection. If you wish, you could stop reading and try to focus for a moment on your feelings. Sometimes you do not want to feel the pain, so you try to run away or stay incredibly busy. So, if you choose to, stop, name your feelings, and write them down. Writing, keeping a journal, is a very healthy and healing thing to do. You can be alone with your thoughts and feelings, and by putting them on paper, you can release them from inside of you. You may not feel like writing right now, so you can always come back to the journal. You may wish to list words or phrases that tell how you feel. You may want to write a letter to your unborn child and say what is in your heart. Here are a few statements to start you on your way if you would find that helpful.

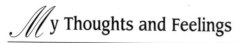

$\mathscr{M}$y Thoughts and Feelings

When I found out I was pregnant with you, I felt _____

_____

_____

_____

_____

_____.

I feel so very empty _____

_____

_____

_____

_____.

$\mathscr{E}$motions

You may feel as if you are on an emotional roller coaster. The sadness and emptiness, anger, guilt, depression, confusion, and fear are all part of those peaks and valleys. You may feel certain emotions intensely and others not at all. Let us take a closer look at some of these feelings.

Sadness and Emptiness

You are so sad and disappointed. It hurts so much and you feel so empty. Your sadness is real. It is not only emotional but may also be physical. One woman told me her arms just ached and felt so empty. She longed to hold her child. She had no appetite even though her stomach felt empty. The woman placed her hands on her stomach and spoke out loud, as if speaking directly to her child, "I know it is my womb that is really empty, because you are no longer growing within me."

You may feel shaky, weak, and in need of bed rest for a few days. Your body must adjust and reset any hormonal imbalance. Grieving is an emotionally draining experience, so you may be depleted of energy.

In addition to the physical and emotional effects, there are also some psychological effects. Some couples prepare the baby's room and buy the crib and other baby supplies early in the pregnancy. This empty room or crib just reinforces the emptiness inside you. If need be, you may want to put the things away, possibly after you have touched them, cried over them, and acknowledged the feelings they stir in you.

There may be other reminders of your loss. You may see pregnant women or newborn babies. You may walk into a store, see exhibits for baby products, and become hysterical. Be aware that a TV commercial, a song, an anniversary date, or a multitude of things may trigger a memory in you and cause you to become emotional. You are not losing your mind. Try to reassure yourself that these reactions are quite normal. Someone once said that abnormal behavior (crying or emotional outbursts) in this abnormal situation (the loss of the baby) is very normal. You probably planned to conceive, have a healthy pregnancy, and deliver a happy, healthy baby. Even though we know that one pregnancy in five may end in miscarriage, that thought or possibility was not in your consciousness. So, this time of grieving may indeed feel strange (abnormal) for you.

Because of the physical aches and the feelings of emptiness, sometimes it helps to "soothe your soul" by pampering yourself. Take a warm bath, get a manicure or pedicure, or enjoy a facial. A body massage can be a wonderful time of intimacy for you and your spouse to share and nurture each other. Cuddle together in front of a warm fireplace. If none is available, a candle can be safely used for atmosphere. Cuddle whenever you can as you comfort each other. Do something that is good for you. Make healthy choices for your body, mind, spirit, and emotions. Be kind and gentle with yourself.

My Thoughts and Feelings

Now that you are gone, I feel _____

_____

_____

_____

_____.

When I see or hear _____

_____

_____

_____.

ANGER

The waves of feelings keep washing over you. "Why me? Why my baby? Why did this happen to me? Why, God? Why did my body let me down? Why didn't I try to conceive earlier? Why was I so interested in my career?"

Usually you cannot find answers to these Why questions, and this may anger you. You feel angry at the intense disappointment and devastation you are experiencing, or just angry that you even have to feel this pain. Your anger may be directed toward God, your partner, or others who seem to be indifferent to your pain and who may be saying insensitive or inappropriate things.

It is only in recent years that some women have become more open, or have given themselves permission to speak openly about their miscarriage. I have heard such stories of unresolved grief that women have carried with them for years—grief that was not recognized, not "appropriate" to talk about, or just too painful to share. You may feel extremely angry because you have had other miscarriages and you hoped and believed this baby would live. You may feel hurt, resentful, or jealous when you see other women still pregnant and you are not. Whatever you are feeling is real, it is okay, because feelings just *are.* Feelings are not right or wrong; you just feel what you feel. It is the way you express your feelings that determines their release and their effects on you.

One helpful way to release anger is to do something physical: aerobic exercise, walking, bowling, dancing, or playing racquetball—all, of course, after getting your doctor's approval. Your body may need some time to rest and recuperate. Be gentle with yourself. Another suggestion for anger release is to write it out. Write to the person (you need not mail it) or to the circumstance, or just write down how you feel. Here are a few starter statements.

*M*y Thoughts and Feelings

I feel so angry that _____

_____

_____.

I feel angry when _____

_____

_____.

GUILT

Sometimes you turn your anger inward toward yourself, and this may lead to feelings of guilt or depression. The miscarriage has left you feeling shocked. You never dreamed this would happen to you. You may start to blame yourself for doing something wrong. You may begin a "litany" of "I should have," "I would have," "I must have done something to cause this." Shame, blame, and guilt seem to be ingrained in us since childhood. If something doesn't turn out, it must be our fault. Many of us like to be in control of our choices and our destiny. Experts claim that reality is still the major cause of distress and that many things happen over which we have no control. This was out of your control. It was not your fault. Guilt is a judgment you put on yourself. Try to free yourself of any blame or guilt, as it only adds an additional burden of pain to the grief you are already suffering. Try to find out as much information as you can about miscarriages.

If you have unanswered questions, check with your health-care professionals to see if you can find a solution rather than stay in self-doubt and self-blame.

$\mathscr{M}$y Thoughts and Feelings

I feel _____

_____

_____.

I'll ask my doctor _____

_____

_____.

DEPRESSION

Julie had two young children who needed her love and attention, and she did not "feel like" paying attention to them. "I feel so down, so deflated, so robbed. I don't want to do anything or go anywhere. I really don't care." The truth is that life does go on and that many times you do not have the luxury to deal with one thing at a time. Julie knew of other moms who had had a miscarriage, but they seemed to handle it differently. Some women quickly get back on their feet and thrust themselves into their work or daily routine. It is important that you feel what *you* feel and that you do not compare yourself with or to others.

Depression does have a physical effect on your body. Your immune system is lowered and you feel lethargic. The last thing you want to do is get up and be active, and yet, that is a very healthy thing to do. Do something physical. When you can, go for a walk or do one of the exercises mentioned earlier. Exercise can reduce stress and activate your immune system. Exercise releases endorphins, good chemicals in your brain, that can help you feel a little better. Remember to check with your doctor first before you begin an exercise program.

If you find your depression is totally crippling you and it is lasting for an extended period of time, you may want to seek professional help. Some depression is very normal; but if you cannot sleep or eat, if you have lost all interest in the things you like, if you are crying constantly and you cannot function, you may be suffering a deeper depression. There may be additional things happening in your life that are compounding your depression.

Remember that it is a sign of strength, not weakness, to reach out for the help you need.

ROBBED

Many women express the feeling of being robbed after experiencing the death of their baby.

The word *bereaved* means "to be robbed of," "deprived." You have been robbed of your dreams and of your baby. You may feel violated and deprived because you feel your body has let you down. You may long for some form of restitution, some way to fill this empty void inside of you. For now you must deal with the reality of the loss and just be with the pain.

*M*y Thoughts and Feelings

I feel robbed of _____

_____

_____

_____.

I wish _____

_____

_____

_____.

CONFUSION

When you experience a loss, your power of concentration is affected. Ordinary routine tasks become difficult to do. You may feel disorganized, forgetful, and confused. The rug has been pulled out from under you, and this miscarriage has been a shock to your psyche. Be gentle with yourself. Write yourself messages. Write out your "to do" list and cross things off as you complete them. This period of confusion usually lasts for only a little while. It is normal and you can and will get through it.

FEAR

When you experience a trauma or a crisis in your life, you begin to doubt and question yourself. You become fearful of things that never bothered you before. Your mental messages (your self-talk) are frightening you. You may be experiencing mild panic attacks. Sometimes these attacks may come from feeling out of control. You may fear you will never be able to have a child. You may be reluctant or apprehensive to make love, for fear you may conceive and this could happen again. You may even fear that something may happen to your other children.

Fears are normal; but you need to name them, face them, and try to get through them. You need to talk about them out loud. Talk to your husband, your family and friends, and your doctor about your concerns. Talk to others who have experienced a fetal death and find out how they have dealt with their fears and pain. Name and acknowledge what you worry about and fear the most.

Ask your partner to share his concerns with you. Talk to your children about their fears.

$\mathscr{M}$y Thoughts and Feelings

I really worry that _____

_____

_____

_____.

My biggest fear is _____

_____

_____

_____.

$\mathscr{S}$iblings

If you have children, you need to know that they also grieve. They need to feel loved, safe, and reassured. If you have told them of the pregnancy, it is important that they know about the miscarriage. Children are resilient and will follow your lead and example. They may be very disappointed, confused, and sad at the loss of their sibling. They need to understand what happened, and they also need to be encouraged to share their fears, thoughts, and feelings. Sometimes it helps, when age appropriate, to invite the children to write letters to the baby or to draw pictures of the family or pictures that express their feelings. Children need to be included in whatever ceremonial rituals you have as a family, and to share in the family's expression of grief.

Children are extremely perceptive. They pick up your moods, feelings, and vibrations. They will know something is wrong, so do not hide the truth from them. They will be sensitive to your grieving and will probably attempt to "fix" you and "make it all better." Teach them it is okay for you to cry and be sad, because that is how you are feeling right now. You are a role model. It will be an excellent life lesson for them to learn about loss and to gain an understanding of grief. Most of us were never taught about grief or how to deal with it.

*F*amily and Friends

As mentioned earlier, other people may not recognize your pain. They may be insensitive to you or may not know what to say or do. They may be uncomfortable around you because you remind them that they, too, are vulnerable. It may be a beneficial lesson in communication for them if you share honestly about how you feel. Tell them you have had a miscarriage, you are very sad, and it hurts very much. Let them know that it would be a help to you if they could allow you to speak about it openly. By expressing what you need and asking for support, you can help yourself and encourage others to be open and to respond to you in whatever way they can.

*Y*our Spouse

Hopefully, you and your spouse are sharing and grieving together. He may or may not know how you are feeling. He may sense your pain and, hopefully, be supportive. He may also be in pain yet feel frustrated because he is helpless and not able to "fix" you or the situation. He may be grieving in his own way. Whatever dreams he had for his baby have also been shattered. He may not know how to be there for you, or he may withdraw emotionally. He may not understand and yet insist that you feel better and move on, now. You both may have some very mixed emotions about the pregnancy and the miscarriage. There may be some hidden sense of relief or certain unexpressed fears; for example, Were we ready for a baby? Would we be good parents? Could we afford to start our family now? You both need to discuss your feelings and share as best you can. You need to ask him for what you need and possibly guide him through the experience with you. He cannot read your mind, and he may believe he has to be in charge and take your pain away.

In our society, men are the forgotten grievers. Most people will ask a man, "How's your wife doing?" "Tell her we're thinking about her and we are so sorry to hear what happened." Men need support too—"big boys can and do cry." Tears are good. When we cry tears from emotion, toxins are released from our bodies. Dads need permission to cry too. They need to ask for what they want. They should be encouraged to share their feelings and to reach out to other fathers whose baby has died. It is a sign of strength, not weakness, for men and women to face the pain, feel it, express it, walk through it, and come out on the other side of it. It is also a sign of strength to ask for what you need.

$\mathcal{S}$haring Together

It is a common belief that a tragedy brings a couple closer together. History and statistics show us that this is not always true. The death of a child is the hardest reality a couple must face. It is imperative that you both continue to communicate and to work on your relationship. It is important that you do not isolate or shut each other out. Sometimes spouses grieve alone and one is afraid of upsetting the other and causing more pain. Sometimes you both bury yourself in your work or stay incredibly busy so the feelings will not surface. Share your grief, your tears. Talk about your feelings and remember your dreams and family plans. Whenever you can, laugh together and try to enjoy the lighter moments that occur. A sense of humor can help pull you through the trying times. Your mutual love and respect can be a great comfort during this time of sadness. You need to be together to feel that love, warmth, and closeness, especially as you express your feelings about making love again. You need to listen to each other, validate and accept each other's feelings. Encourage each other to express any fears or concerns and continue to let go of any blame or guilt. Together you need to meet with your health-care professionals to discuss any questions about the miscarriage and any concerns you have about getting pregnant again.

My Thoughts and Feelings

Together we can _____

_____

_____

_____.

One thing I love about our relationship is _____

_____

_____

_____.

Ceremonies of Healing

What can you do when it seems there is nothing that can be done? When you are ready, you can do something that will be of help to you. Ceremonies are acts or rituals that can be used to help you express your feelings and remember those you love. These memories are very difficult to deal with in the beginning, but they are treasured later on and they do last a lifetime. You will never forget the child of your womb.

Miscarriage occurs at various stages of fetal development. The age of your baby at the time of death may determine your choice of ceremonies. You may have held your small child in your hand or arms to say good-bye, or you may have been able to say good-bye without seeing or holding your baby. At this time, you may believe that you will never be able to completely say good-bye.

Here are a few ideas of ceremonies that have helped others express their grief and create some type of a memorial to the one they love. This is not an exhaustive list, so you are strongly encouraged to design a ceremony or memorial that is meaningful to you.

You may have—

* had a formal burial.

* had a tombstone or a plaque inscribed with the baby's name and date of death.

* had a religious ceremony.

* lit a candle and prayed a favorite prayer, psalm, or poem.

* named the baby.

* written letters to the baby at different times and later buried or burned the letters.

* planted a tree, a bush, flowers, a garden, or an herb garden.

* made a special wreath, bouquet, or ornament.

* written and created a memory book with songs or poems.

* donated to a special cause for children.

* volunteered to help children in a hospital or day-care center.

* invited others to share with you, or you may have conducted your ceremony or memorial in private.
* created your own meaningful ways to help you remember.

$\mathscr{M}$y Thoughts and Feelings

I would find it helpful to _____

_____

_____

_____

_____

_____

_____.

My way to remember _____

_____

_____

_____

_____

_____

_____.

Remember and Release

Only a person who avoids the joy of love in life will be able to avoid the pain of grief in death. When you love so intensely and that love is lost, you miss it so intensely. You will always remember the child in your womb. Your miscarriage and the pain you feel have changed you and your life. The suffering you feel is real, but according to parents who have lived through the experience, the pain does lessen. You can go on and eventually you do heal, but the scar will always remain.

There was no choice in the death of your baby, but you do have a choice about how you will deal with the pain and how you will continue to live and love again.

Remember that your journey through grief is hard work and it does take time. It cannot nor should not be avoided, because unresolved grief does affect your life and it can keep you in pain. Memories, whether painful or joyful, will always be a part of you and will surface at unexpected times. As we said, memories can be very painful, but it is those very memories that give you great comfort later on. Remember the love you felt for that child in your womb? No one, not even the pain or grief, can ever take that away from you. Remember those who have helped you, shared with you, and listened to you, and those whom you have helped during this time. You do not have all the answers, and you do not always have to say the right words. You probably now realize that no one can take away the pain of others, but you know the comfort you felt when others were there for you. Remember that life is filled with change, loss, love, growth, and challenges, and you have a choice in the way you handle these. Remember that your powerful human spirit can walk through pain and can change and soar to a higher level of growth and potential. Your love and healing is your testimony to this power within you.

Be gentle with yourself as you continue your journey through life, love, and healing.

_M_y Thoughts and Feelings

I remember _____

_____

_____

_____

_____

_____.

I choose _____

_____

_____

_____

_____

_____.

My Thoughts and Feelings

My Thoughts and Feelings

ESOURCES

Centering Corporation
1531 N. Saddle Creek Road
Omaha, NE 68103
402-553-1200; Fax 402-553-0507

> Provides supportive materials for people experiencing
> crisis such as death of a child.

Compassionate Friends
National Office, P.O. Box 3696
Oak Brook, IL 60522-3696
708-990-0010; Fax 708-990-0246

> This self-help organization offers support, friendship, and
> understanding to bereaved parents. It holds a monthly
> support-group meeting and usually publishes a monthly
> newsletter.

National SHARE
St. Joseph's Health Center
30 First Capital Drive
St. Charles, MO 63301
314-947-5000

> Provides support for bereaved parents who have suffered
> a miscarriage or infant death. This organization publishes
> a newsletter and a listing of national support groups.

Pails of Hope
(Pregnancy and Parenting after Infertility/Loss)
For information contact Pen Parents, Inc.
Phone and Fax 702-826-7332

> A newsletter for bereaved parents, published six times a
> year.

Pen Parents, Inc.
P.O. Box 8738
Reno, NV 89507-8738
Phone and Fax 702-826-7332

A nonprofit international correspondence network for
bereaved parents after pregnancy loss or the death of a
child of any age. *Heart Songs,* a journal for grieving
parents, professionals, and interested persons, is
published quarterly by this organization.

Perinatal Loss
2116 N.E. 18th Street
Portland, OR 97212
503-264-7426; Fax 503-282-8985

Provides books and resources for parents and grandparents after a miscarriage, a stillbirth, or an infant death.

A Place to Remember
1885 University Avenue, Suite 110
St. Paul, MN 55104
612-476-1303

A division of deRutyer Nelson Publications, Inc., providing
booklets and other resources for bereaved parents and
grandparents.

Resolve, Inc.
P.O. Box 474
Belmont, MA 02178
617-484-2424

Offers telephone support, a newsletter, support groups,
and information on infertility.

Unite of Jeanes Hospital
7600 Central Avenue
Philadelphia, PA 19111
215-728-2000

> Provides support groups, a newsletter, support for
> bereaved parents, and education to professionals.

Wintergreen Press, Inc.
3630 Eileen Street
Maple Plain, MN 55359
612-476-1303

> Wintergreen Press publishes and distributes resources for
> the bereaved and professionals who deal with
> bereavement.

OOKS

Arnold, Joan Hagan, and Penelope Buschman Jemma. *A Child
Dies: A Portrait of Family Grief.* Rockville, Md.: Aspen
System Corporation, 1983.

Ilse, Sherokee. *Empty Arms: A Guide to Help Parents and Loved
Ones Cope with Miscarriage, Stillbirth, and Newborn Death.*
Maple Plain, Minn.: Wintergreen Press, 1982.

Jimenez, Sherry Lynn Mims. *The Other Side of Pregnancy:
Coping with Miscarriage and Stillbirth.* Englewood Cliffs,
N.J.: Prentice Hall, Inc., 1983.

Keaggy, Bernadette. *A Deeper Shade of Grace.* Nashville,
Tenn.: Sparrow Press, 1993.

Kushner, Rabbi Harold S. *When Bad Things Happen to Good
People.* New York: Schoeken Books, 1981.

Manning, Doug. *Don't Take My Grief Away.* New York: Harper
& Row, 1984.

Schiff, Harriet S. *The Bereaved Parent.* New York: Penguin
Books, 1978.